Sea

Series "Fun Facts on Water Animals for Kids"

Written by Michelle Hawkins

Seal

Series "Fun Facts on Ocean Animals for Kids"
By: Michelle Hawkins
Version 1.1 ~August 2021
Published by Michelle Hawkins at KDP
Copyright ©2021 by Michelle Hawkins. All rights reserved.

No part of this publication may be reproduced, distributed or transmitted in any form or by any means including photocopying, recording or other electronic or mechanical methods or by any information storage or retrieval system without the prior written permission of the publishers, except in the case of very brief quotations embodied in critical reviews and certain other noncommercial uses permitted by copyright law.

All rights reserved, including the right of reproduction in whole or in part in any form.

All information in this book has been carefully researched and checked for factual accuracy. However, the author and publisher make no warranty, express or implied, that the information contained herein is appropriate for every individual, situation, or purpose and assume no responsibility for errors or omissions.

The reader assumes the risk and full responsibility for all actions. The author will not be held responsible for any loss or damage, whether consequential, incidental, special or otherwise, that may result from the information presented in this book.

All images are free for use or purchased from stock photo sites or royalty-free for commercial use. I have relied on my own observations as well as many different sources for this book, and I have done my best to check facts and give credit where it is due. In the event that any material is used without proper permission, please contact me so that the oversight can be corrected.

Seals are born with a fur coat.

When a Seal goes across the ice, it can move up to 15 miles per hour.

Seals will hunt in groups or by themselves.

The highest population of Seals is found in the Arctic and Antarctic.

Seals are considered threatened.

Seals will eat 5% of their body weight each day.

It is hard for a Seal to walk on land due to its flippers.

The milk that a mom gives to a baby Seal is 50% fat to help build blubber on a Seal.

Seals do not have tear ducts, so they are unable to cry.

Seals can migrate yearly in search of food.

Seals are related to bears.

The Galapagos Fur Seal is considered endangered.

Seals are mammals.

When Seals swim, they look like they are gliding through the water.

Some Seals can dive over 300 yards looking for food in the water.

Seals use their whiskers and eyesight to help them catch food.

March 22nd is International Seal Day.

Many people say Seals are clowns because they enjoy clowning around.

There are over 30 different types of Seals in the world.

Seals can open and close their tail.

Seals can swim up to 22 miles per hour.

The Elephant Seal is the largest in the world at 16 feet long and up to 7,000 pounds.

Seals are known to be very territorial.

The only freshwater seal is the Baikal Seal.

On land, Seal will live in colonies with each other.

Seals can range from 100 pounds to 7,000 pounds.

Female Seals are called Cows.

The flippers on the back of a Seal are smaller than their front flippers.

A baby Seal can walk and swim within a few hours of being born.

Seals are considered to be a warm-blooded creatures.

Female Seals will give birth to one Seal at a time.

The only time Seals are fully asleep is when they are on land.

Seals live between 25 to 30 years.

Depending on the type of Seal, they are pregnant 10 to 14 months.

Seals have great hearing underwater.

All breeds of Seals (except one) can be found in saltwater.

Seals live in water but need air to breathe.

When diving, Seals can make their heartbeat slow down to 4 to 6 beats per minute.

A baby seal is called a pup.

Seals are known to be aggressive.

When looking for food, Seals are known to travel up to 30 miles per day.

Female Seals tend to live longer than male Seals.

The favorite food of Seals is fish and squid.

Seals can hold their breath underwater longer than any other mammal.

Certain types of Seals can hold their breath underwater for up to two hours.

The most populated Seal in the world is the Crabeater Seal.

Seals can not see in color.

Seals have excellent eyesight.

Seals can be from three to sixteen feet in length.

A mother and baby Seal will always recognize each other through sound.

Seals can regulate their body temperature to keep warm.

The ears of a Seal do not stick out.

You can tell a male Seal by their fat nose.

A male Seal is called a bull.

Seals can sleep underwater.

When sleeping underwater, only have of their brain is asleep.

The Galapagos Fur Seal is the smallest Seal at three feet and 100 pounds.

The mom Seal is continually teaching their babies how to swim better.

There is more blood in a Seal on average than any other animal.

Seals can swim in both cold and warm water.

Seals will use their flippers to help them move across the ice.

Most baby Seals are born between February to July.

Seals communicate with each other by clicking and whistling.

When born, a baby Seal can weigh between 10 to 50 pounds.

The heart rate of a Seal on land is 75 to 120 beats per minute.

Seals can live on the water as well as on the land.

The eyes on a Seal are large and round.

An Elephant Seal can hold its breath for up to two hours underwater.

Seals can hold their breath underwater by slowing down their heart rate.

As baby Seal, they can put on up to four pounds of weight per day.

The whiskers on a Seal are very sensitive to their environment.

Baby Seals are independent of their mother by the age of two.

Seals can see in the blue and green spectrum.

Seals do not have legs, only flippers.

The Monk Seal is the state animal of Hawaii.

Seals can see great in the nighttime.

Seals belong to the group Pinnipeds.

The male Seal will dance to attract a female Seal.

Seals, on average, are only underwater for three minutes at a time.

The blubber under a Seal's skin allows them to keep warm.

A group of Seals is called a colony or a raft.

Seals come in the colors of black, brown, and gray.

Seals are carnivores; they only eat fish and meat.

The whiskers on a Seal help to sense vibrations in the water to help them find food.

Find me on Amazon at:

https://amzn.to/3oqoXoG

and on Facebook at:

https://bit.ly/3ovFJ5V

Other Books by Michelle Hawkins

Series

Fun Facts on Birds for Kids.

Fun Fact on Fruits and Vegetables

Fun Facts on Small Animals

Fun Facts on Dogs for Kids.

Fun Facts on Dates for Kids.

Fun Facts on Zoo Animals for Kids

Fun Facts on Farm Animals for Kids

Fun Facts on Ocean Animals for Kids.

10% of all profits are donated to World Vision at https://rb.gy/cahrb0

Printed in Great Britain
by Amazon